Easy

Origami

Greeting Cards

by Christopher Harbo

CAPSTONE PRESS
a capstone imprint

First Facts are published by Capstone Press,
1710 Roe Crest Drive, North Mankato, Minnesota 56003
www.mycapstone.com

Library of Congress Cataloging-in-Publication Data
Names: Harbo, Christopher L., author.
Title: Easy origami greeting cards : an augmented reality crafting experience / by
    Christopher Harbo.
Description: North Mankato, Minnesota : Capstone Press, 2017. | Series: First facts.
    Origami crafting 4D | Includes bibliographical references. | Audience: Ages 6–9. |
    Audience: Grades K to 3.
Identifiers: LCCN 2016044990| ISBN 9781515735878 (library binding) |
    ISBN 9781515735922 (ebook (pdf)
Subjects: LCSH: Origami—Juvenile literature. | Greeting cards—Juvenile literature.
Classification: LCC TT872.5 .H3734 2017 | DDC 736/.982—dc23
LC record available at https://lccn.loc.gov/2016044990

Summary: Provides photo-illustrated instructions for making five origami models and three craft projects. Also includes embedded video links for online instructional tutorials that can be accessed with the Capstone 4D app.

Editorial Credits
Sarah Bennett, designer; Laura Manthe, production specialist

The author thanks Rachel Walwood for designing and creating all of the origami craft projects in this book.

Photo Credits
Photographs and design elements by Capstone Studio: Karon Dubke. Line drawings by Capstone: Sandra D'Antonio. Additional design elements: Shutterstock: Ammak, Lena Bukovsky

Table of Contents

Crafty Origami Greeting Cards

A well-folded origami model is a treasure all by itself. But place it on a greeting card, and your tiny paper masterpiece will surely draw smiles. Surprise a friend with a pop-up invitation that features paper teacups and lanterns. Or send a delightful thank-you note with an origami duck pond theme. The variety of origami greeting cards you can create is endless. Best of all, there are no limits on your crafting creativity!

Download the Capstone 4D App!

Videos for every fold and craft are now at your fingertips with the Capstone 4D app.

To download the Capstone 4D app:
- Search in the Apple App Store or Google Play for "Capstone 4D"
- Click *Install* (Android) or *Get*, then *Install* (Apple)
- Open the application
- Scan any page with this icon

You can also access the additional resources on the web at **www.capstone4D.com** using the password **fold.card**

Materials

Origami is great for crafting because the materials don't cost much. Below are the basic supplies you'll use to complete the projects in this book.

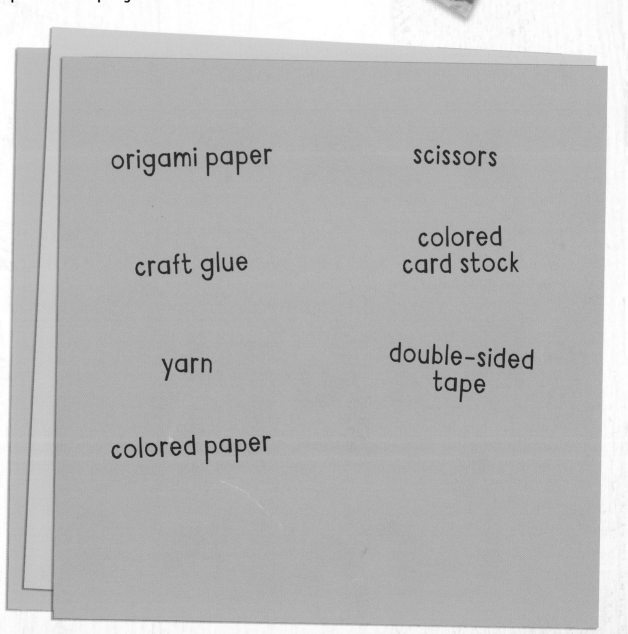

origami paper

scissors

craft glue

colored card stock

yarn

double-sided tape

colored paper

Terms and Techniques

Folding paper is easier when you understand basic origami folding terms and symbols. Practice the folds below before trying the models in this book.

Valley folds are represented by a dashed line. One side of the paper is folded against the other like a book.

Mountain folds are represented by a dashed and dotted line. The paper is folded sharply behind the model.

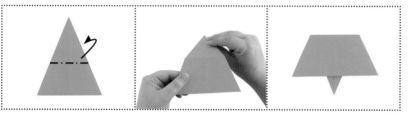

Squash folds are formed by lifting one edge of a pocket. The pocket gets folded again so the spine gets flattened. The existing fold lines become new edges.

Inside reverse folds are made by opening a pocket slightly. Then you fold the model inside itself along the fold lines or existing creases.

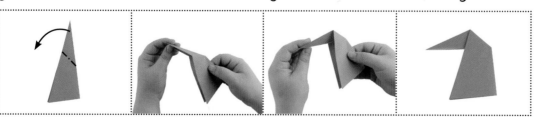

Outside reverse folds are made by opening a pocket slightly. Then you fold the model outside itself along the fold lines or existing creases.

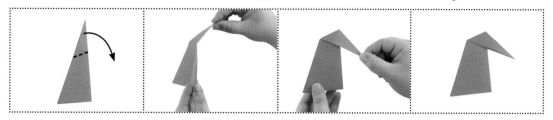

Rabbit ear folds are formed by bringing two edges of a point together using existing fold lines. The new point is folded to one side.

Pleat folds are made by using both a mountain fold and a valley fold.

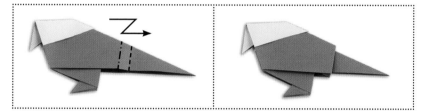

Symbols

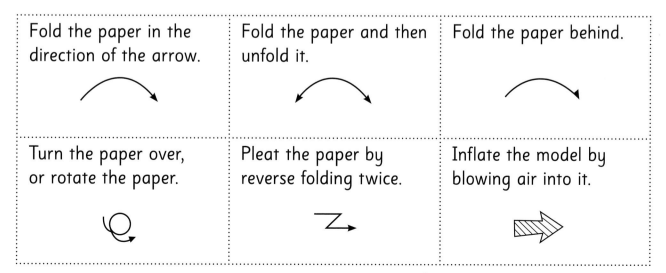

Fold the paper in the direction of the arrow.	Fold the paper and then unfold it.	Fold the paper behind.
Turn the paper over, or rotate the paper.	Pleat the paper by reverse folding twice.	Inflate the model by blowing air into it.

Hen

Here's a rare origami model that uses the white side of the paper for its main color. This hen only needs a flash of red to proudly strut her stuff.

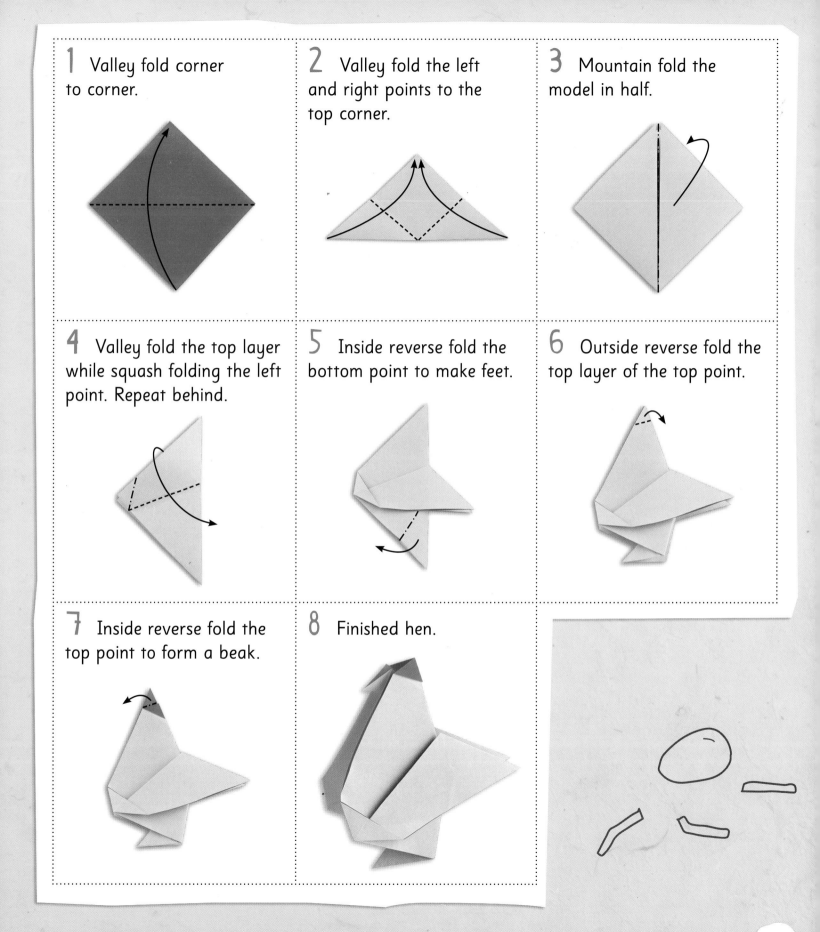

1 Valley fold corner to corner.

2 Valley fold the left and right points to the top corner.

3 Mountain fold the model in half.

4 Valley fold the top layer while squash folding the left point. Repeat behind.

5 Inside reverse fold the bottom point to make feet.

6 Outside reverse fold the top layer of the top point.

7 Inside reverse fold the top point to form a beak.

8 Finished hen.

Pig

With its little snout and tail, there is only one way to make this paper porker cuter. Fold it in pretty pink or peach paper.

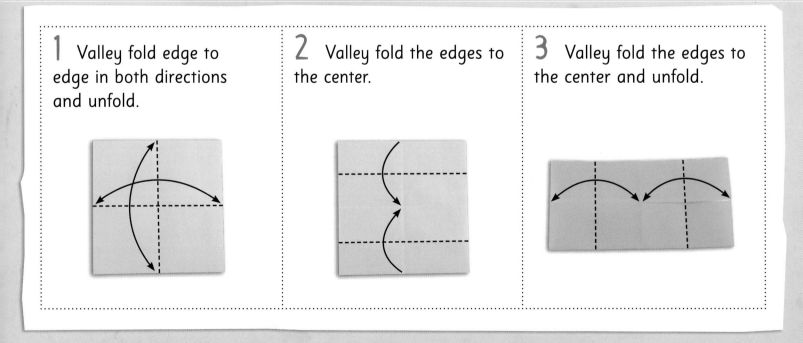

1 Valley fold edge to edge in both directions and unfold.

2 Valley fold the edges to the center.

3 Valley fold the edges to the center and unfold.

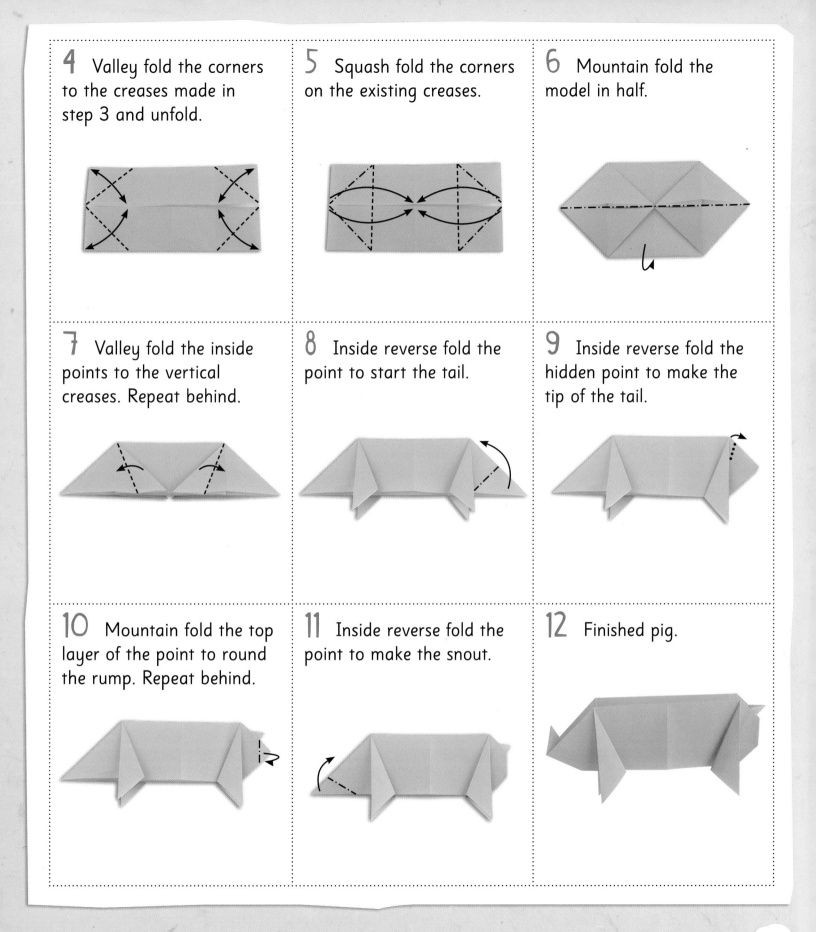

4 Valley fold the corners to the creases made in step 3 and unfold.

5 Squash fold the corners on the existing creases.

6 Mountain fold the model in half.

7 Valley fold the inside points to the vertical creases. Repeat behind.

8 Inside reverse fold the point to start the tail.

9 Inside reverse fold the hidden point to make the tip of the tail.

10 Mountain fold the top layer of the point to round the rump. Repeat behind.

11 Inside reverse fold the point to make the snout.

12 Finished pig.

Barnyard Card

Build a barnyard card that would make Old McDonald proud. It's the perfect setting for your origami pigs and hens.

What You Need

8.5- by 11-inch (22- by 28-centimeter) sheet of red card stock

scissors

double-sided tape

13 6-inch (15-cm) strips of white card stock

.75- by 1-inch (2- by 2.5-cm) piece of red card stock

1- by 1.25-inch (2.5- by 3.2-cm) piece of white card stock

large origami hen

3 small origami hens

2 origami pigs

*fold the pigs and large hen from 4-inch (10.2-cm) squares, and the small hens from 3-inch (7.6-cm) squares

What You Do

1 Fold the red sheet of card stock in half so the long edges meet. Unfold.

2 Cut the card stock in half along the crease made in step 1. Set one half aside.

3 Fold the piece of card stock you kept in half so the short edges meet. Unfold.

4 Fold the sides of the card stock to the crease made in step 3. Set aside the doors of your barn.

5 Pick up the other piece of card stock you set aside in step 2. Cut out a barn roof shape. Make the base of the roof wide enough to match the width of the doors.

6 Tape the doors to the base of the roof.

7 Tape strips of white card stock around the edges of the doors and roof. Trim off any extra strips that extend beyond the edges of the card.

8 Tape the small red rectangle of card stock on top of the slightly larger white rectangle of card stock. Tape this small door to the barn's roof.

9 Tape the origami hens and pigs anywhere you like inside and outside the barn to complete your card.

Teacup

Tea plays an important role in Japanese culture. This model represents the simple beauty of a traditional teacup.

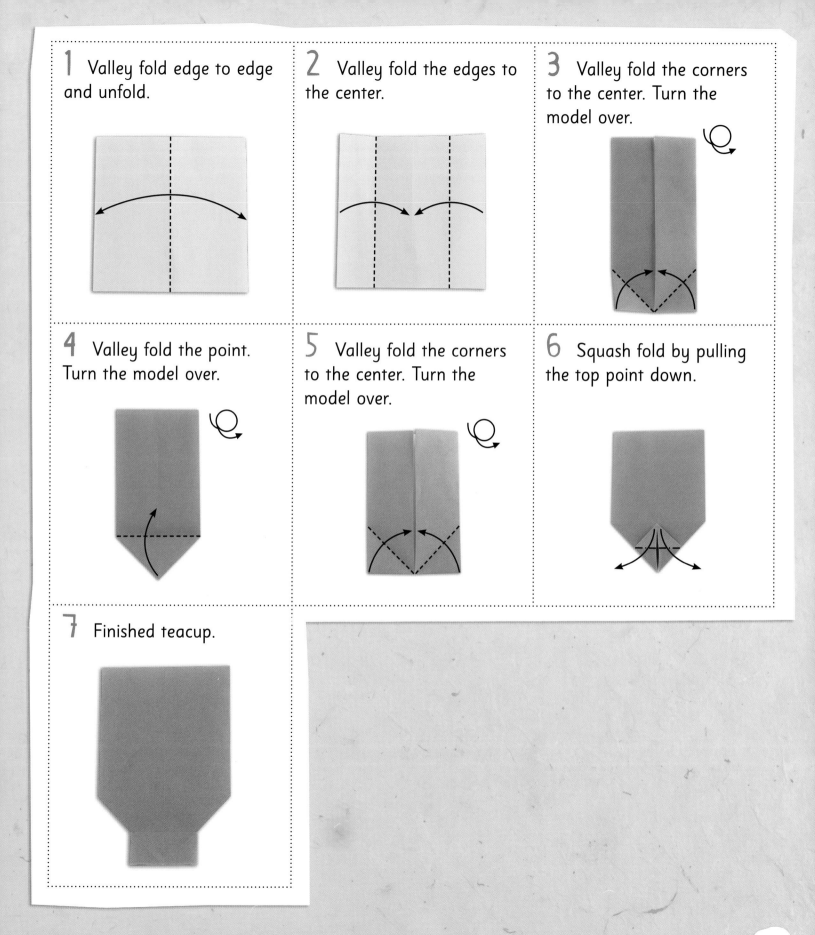

1 Valley fold edge to edge and unfold.

2 Valley fold the edges to the center.

3 Valley fold the corners to the center. Turn the model over.

4 Valley fold the point. Turn the model over.

5 Valley fold the corners to the center. Turn the model over.

6 Squash fold by pulling the top point down.

7 Finished teacup.

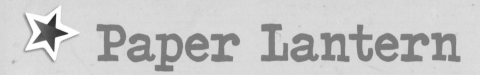

Paper Lantern

In Japan and China, paper lanterns often light up celebrations and festivals. They are also hung outside businesses to attract customers.

1 Valley fold edge to edge in both directions and unfold.

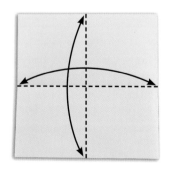

2 Valley fold the edges to the center.

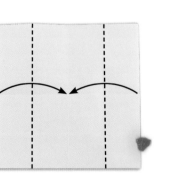

3 Valley fold the corners to the center.

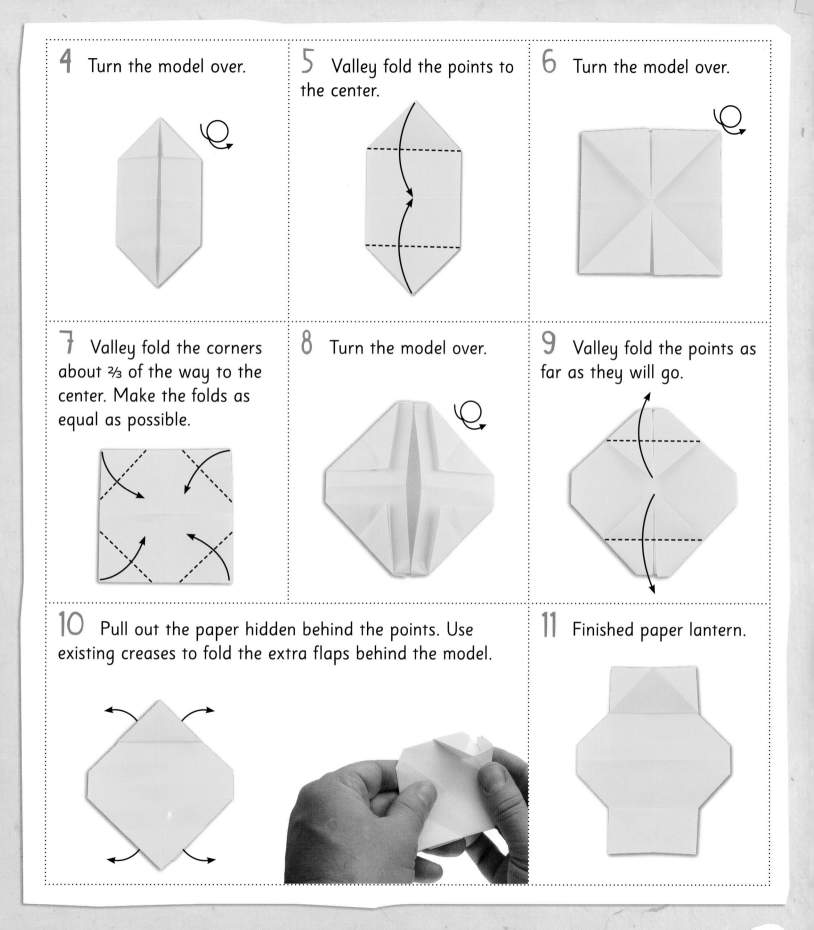

4 Turn the model over.

5 Valley fold the points to the center.

6 Turn the model over.

7 Valley fold the corners about ⅔ of the way to the center. Make the folds as equal as possible.

8 Turn the model over.

9 Valley fold the points as far as they will go.

10 Pull out the paper hidden behind the points. Use existing creases to fold the extra flaps behind the model.

11 Finished paper lantern.

Tea Shop Card

Make origami greeting cards that burst with surprises!
Use origami lanterns and teacups to create an
amazing pop-up tea shop card.

What You Need

8.5- by 11-inch (21.6- by 28-cm)
   sheet of green card stock

6- by 3.5-inch (15- by 9-cm)
   piece of brown card stock

craft glue

2 origami teacups

5 origami lanterns

8.5-inch (21.6-cm) long
   piece of yarn

*fold the teacups and lanterns from
   3-inch (7.6-cm) squares

What You Do

1 Fold the green sheet of card stock in
   half so the short edges meet. Set the
   card aside.

2 Fold narrow flaps on both short
   edges of the brown piece of card stock.
   Then fold the piece of card stock in half
   so the flaps meet. This will be your
   pop-up table.

3 Glue the flaps of the pop-up table inside
   the card so the table folds and unfolds
   when the card is opened and closed. Be
   sure to line up the bottom of the table
   with the bottom edge of the card. Allow
   to dry.

4 Glue a small origami teacup to each
   side of the table. Allow to dry.

5 Glue the paper lanterns along the
   length of the yarn. Allow to dry.

6 Glue the string of paper lanterns inside
   the card so it hangs above the table
   when the card is opened. Allow to dry.

Mandarin Duck

The male mandarin duck is known for the "sail" feathers that stick up from his back. This model uses that feature to create a truly unique origami duck.

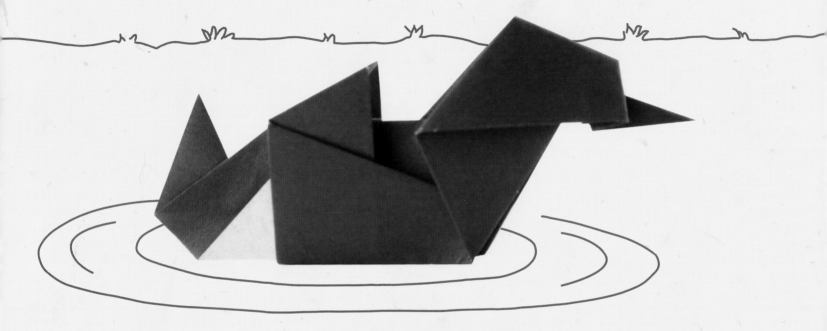

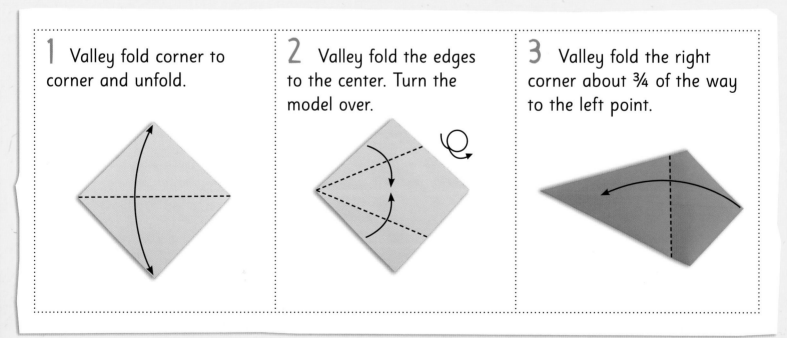

1 Valley fold corner to corner and unfold.

2 Valley fold the edges to the center. Turn the model over.

3 Valley fold the right corner about ¾ of the way to the left point.

4 Valley fold the top flap along the vertical edge.

5 Mountain fold the model in half.

6 Valley fold the top layer so the dot meets the top edge. Repeat behind.

7 Outside reverse fold so the dot meets the top edge.

8 Outside reverse fold the point to make the head.

9 Pleat fold the head to make the beak.

10 Pleat fold the point to make a tail.

11 Finished mandarin duck.

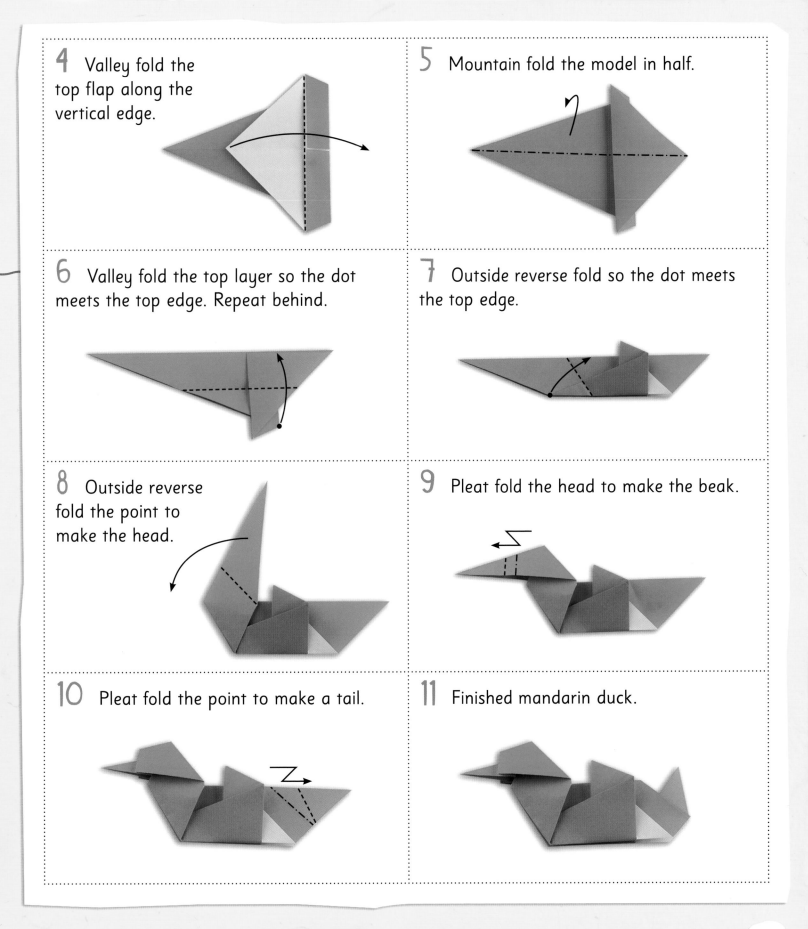

Duck Pond Card

Delight your loved ones with this origami duck pond card.
It's perfect for thank-you notes or invitations to an outdoor party.

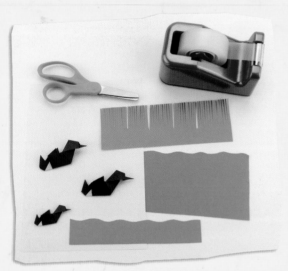

What You Need

5.5- by 7.5-inch (14- by 19-cm)
   piece of tan card stock

scissors

2- by 5.5-inch (5- by 14-cm) piece
   of green paper

double-sided tape

3- by 5.5-inch (7.6- by 14-cm)
   piece of blue paper

1.5- by 5.5-inch (4- by 14-cm)
   piece of blue paper

2 large origami ducks

small origami duck

*fold the large ducks from 4-inch
   (10.2-cm) squares, and the small
   duck from a 3-inch (7.6-cm) square

What You Do

1 Fold the tan piece of card stock in half so the short edges meet. Set the card aside.

2 Cut narrow slits all along one long edge of the green paper to make grass. Each slit should be about 1 inch (2.5 cm) deep.

3 Tape the green paper to the card. Make the top of the grass even with the folded edge of the card.

4 Cut a wavy line along one long edge of the large blue paper. Make your cut about .5 inch (1.3 cm) in from the edge.

5 Tape the large blue paper to the card. Make the long straight edge of the paper even with the bottom of the card. The wavy edge should now overlap the green grass slightly.

6 Repeat steps 4 and 5 with the small piece of blue paper. Your card should now look like a pond with two sets of waves.

7 Tape the origami ducks anywhere you like on the blue water to complete your duck pond card.

Read More

Claybourne, Anna. *Cards, Wrap, and Tags.* Be Creative. Mankato, Minn.: Smart Apple Media, 2013.

Lim, Annalees. *Decorative Card Crafts.* 10-Minute Crafts. New York: Windmill Books, 2016.

Song, Sok. *Origami Accessories: A Foldable Fashion Guide.* Fashion Origami. North Mankato, Minn.: Capstone Press, 2016.

Turnbull, Stephanie. *Cards and Gifts: Style Secrets for Girls.* Girl Talk. Mankato, Minn.: Smart Apple Media, 2014.

Internet Sites

FactHound offers a safe, fun way to find Internet sites related to this book. All of the sites on FactHound have been researched by our staff.

Here's all you do:
Visit *www.facthound.com*
Type in this code: 9781515735878

Check out projects, games and lots more at
www.capstonekids.com